Text: *Carl Rogers and Steve Goodier*

Series Editor: *Tony Bowerman*

Photographs: *Carl Rogers, Rob Stevens, Tony Bowerman, Dreamstime, Shutterstock*

Design: *Carl Rogers and Laura Hodgkinson*

Northern Eye Books
ISBN 978-1-908632-80-7

A CIP catalogue record for this book is available from the British Library

www.northerneyebooks.co.uk

Cover: Llyn Idwal
(Walk 6) Rob Stevens
Photography

First published in 2020 by:

Northern Eye Books Limited
Northern Eye Books, Tattenhall, Cheshire CH3 9PX
Email: tony@northerneyebooks.co.uk
For sales enquiries, please call: 01928 723 744

MIX
Paper from
responsible sources
FSC® C022174

 Instagram: @northerneyebooks
@Carlrogers1960

 Twitter: @northerneyeboo
@CarlMarabooks

 Facebook: @northerneyebooks

Contents

Snowdonia National Park 4

Top 10 Walks: Snowdonia's best walks 6

1. **Aber Falls**, *waterfall walk* 8

2. **The Erskine Arms**, *pub walk* 14

3. **Llyn Crafnant**, *lakeside walk* 20

4. **Capel Curig,** *viewpoint walk* 26

5. **Harlech beach**, *coastal walk* 32

6. **Llyn Ogwen** & **Idwal,** *lakeside walk* 38

7. **Mynydd Mawr**, *hill walk* 44

8. **Tal y Fan**, *hill walk* 48

9. **Cadair Idris**, *mountain walk* 52

10. **Snowdon**, *mountain walk* 58

Useful Information 64

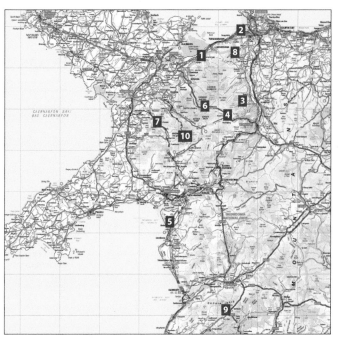

Snowdonia National Park

Snowdonia is one of the most celebrated and spectacular highland areas in the British Isles — a region of hills, lakes, mountains and wild moorland occupying the northwest corner of Wales.

Snowdonia National Park (Parc Cenedlaethol Eryri) was established in 1951 as the third National Park in Britain, following the Peak District and the Lake District. It covers 827 square miles (2,140 square kilometres) and, rather surprisingly, has 37 miles (60 kilometres) of coastline. There is great variety within this small area — the park contains all of Wales' 14 highest mountains, as well as a host of lakes, woods, beautiful valleys and high moorland.

The unique flora and fauna of the area includes rare mammals such as otter, polecat and feral goat. Birds of prey include peregrine, osprey, merlin and red kite, with rare plants like the Arctic-alpine Snowdon lily and the unique Snowdon hawkweed.

Sunset over the Llanberis Pass

The very best of **Snowdonia**

These ten themed walks will take you to the best and most iconic places across the Snowdonia National Park.

Famous for its lofty mountains and open hills, Snowdonia is characterised, too, by dramatic upland lakes and tarns enfolded within glacial troughs and valleys, and short, steep rivers tumbling to the sea.

Discover vast empty beaches, friendly pubs and stunning views, hidden lakes and awesome waterfalls, challenging hills and mighty mountains.

Every one is a walk to enjoy and savour on the day, and remember long afterwards.

"Lovely the woods, waters, meadows, combes, vales,
All the air things wear that build this world of Wales."

Gerard Manley Hopkins

TOP 10 **Walks:** Snowdonia's finest walks

HERE, PACKED INTO A POCKET-SIZE BOOK, are ten of the best short circular walks in the Snowdonia National Park. They've been carefully chosen — from the already popular themed *Top 10 Walks: Snowdonia* series — to showcase the finest and most enjoyable walks across the mountains, hills, lakes and coast of North Wales. So, whether you fancy a stroll to a view, a memorable tour of medieval town walls, a short walk to Wales' highest waterfall, or something more challenging, there's plenty to go at in this little gem of a book.

WATERFALL WALK

Aber Falls

page 8

PUB WALK

Erskine Arms, Conwy

page 14

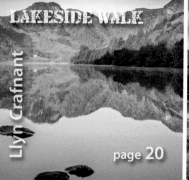

LAKESIDE WALK

Llyn Crafnant

page 20

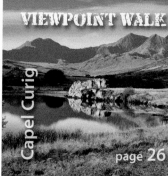

VIEWPOINT WALK

Capel Curig

page 26

COASTAL WALK

Harlech beach

page 32

LAKESIDE WALK

Llyn Idwal & Llyn Ogwen

page 38

HILL WALK

Mynydd Mawr

page 44

HILL WALK

Tal y Fan

page 48

MOUNTAIN WALK

Cadair Idris

page 52

MOUNTAIN WALK

Snowdon/Yr Wyddfa

page 58

The mighty Aber Falls/Rhaeadr Fawr plunges120 feet over an igneous sill

Aber Falls

An atmospheric walk to two of Wales' highest waterfalls set at the head of a deep wooded valley with ancient remains

What to expect:

Surfaced track, viewing areas, grassy paths and a steep descent. Stream crossings, wet in places

Distance/time: 7 kilometres/ 4½ miles. Allow 2½ to 3½ hours

Start: Lower and Upper car parks (pay and display) at Bont Newydd, up signed lane above Abergwyngregyn. Picnic tables, toilets

Grid ref: SH 662 720

Ordnance Survey Map: OS Explorer OL17 Snowdon/Yr Wyddfa - Conwy Valley/Dyffryn Conwy

After the walk: Caffi Hen Felin, Abergwyngregyn LL33 0LP 01248 689454

Walk outline

A broad surfaced path rises from the Bont Newydd car parks through wooded upland meadows, high above the river, to a viewing area below the Aber Falls. Over a footbridge, a path traverses the boggy head of the valley to pass a second, smaller waterfall. The return is on a broad, rising grassy path that undulates along the valley's western flank. Panoramic coastal views lead to a steep descent back to Abegwyngregyn, with its friendly café and lane back up to the car park.

Slate fence at Tŷ Nant

Aber Falls/Rhaeadr Fawr

Just off the narrow coastal strip between Bangor and Llanfairfechan is a hidden, steep-sided wooded valley cut into the northern flanks of the Carneddau mountains by Afon Aber. Two of Wales' highest and most dramatic waterfalls plunge from the cliffs at the head of the valley: Rhaeadr-fawr, the 'great waterfall', and Rhaeadr-fach, the 'little waterfall'. Together they provide the stunning setting for the Coedydd Aber National Nature Reserve whose 114 hectares of river, marsh, oak woods and upland pasture are home to a wealth of wildlife from polecats and otters to kestrels, buzzards, peregrines and ravens.

More walks along the North Wales coast ...

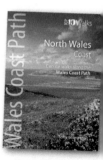

The Walk

1. Leave the two **car parks** on either side of the arched stone bridge at **Bont Newydd** and head up the broad surfaced track on the left bank of **Afon Rhaeadr-fawr**, signed for the **'Aber Falls Walk'**. Go through a gate beside a **circular wooden hut** and follow the track as it winds gently uphill through woodland-fringed meadows high above the river.

The valley is protected as the Coedydd Aber National Nature Reserve. Once far more extensive, the old sessile oak woods that clothe the steep-sided valley are home to a wealth of plants and animals. Look for bluebells, wood anemones, wild garlic, dogs mercury and yellow pimpernel in spring. You may even be lucky enough to glimpse stoats, weasels, bats and even otters. Common birds here include pied flycatchers, wood warblers, dippers, kestrels and ravens.

Less than a kilometre later, the path skirts slate-fenced **Tŷ Nant**, whose indoors **exhibition** explains the valley's long history. *The old farmhouse once sold tea and lemonade to Victorian visitors to the falls.*

This sheltered valley has been settled since prehistoric times and once controlled the coastal strip and ancient crossing to Anglesey over the Lafan Sands. Recent excavations have uncovered a standing stone, Iron Age roundhouses, medieval 'long huts' and a grain drying kiln.

A Coedydd Aber NNR sign overlooks the valley's twin waterfalls

Through another gated meadow, the path narrows before dropping through an iron footgate to the base of the **Aber Falls** — or *Rhaeadr Fawr*. Continue past the **footbridge** here to a **viewing area** directly below the falls.

2. Return to, and turn left over the **footbridge** to climb steps to a second, **higher viewing area** immediately to the right of the falls.

Now retrace your steps and, within 100 metres, go through an iron **footgate** on your left, signed for the 'North Wales Path'. Follow the path alongside a

drystone wall that edges the head of the valley. Less than half a kilometre later, the path drops to another **footbridge** at the foot of a second smaller **waterfall** — *Rhaeadr-bach*. The path then crosses several small streams before curving to the right to head back down the valley.

3. Follow the obvious, **broad grassy path** as it undulates uphill across the valley's western flanks. *Look back for a panorama of the two waterfalls in their magnificent mountain setting.*

When the path forks, take the lower, right-hand path, waymarked for the

Abergwyngregyn and its ancient earthen castle mound

'North Wales Path' and 'Circular Route'. The path climbs steadily across the sloping pastures before passing beneath parallel **power lines**. Beyond a long **strip of conifers**, the grassy track curves to the left, now high above the narrow entrance to the valley below.

Ahead, a broad panorama opens out that spans Anglesey, the Menai Strait, Puffin Island and the Lafan Sands, with Penmaenmawr and the Great Orme away to the right.

4. Follow the track over the brow of the hill to a **field gate**. Once through it, the track forks. Ahead and to the left, the

North Wales Path continues along the top of the slope. Instead, however, turn right here, downhill towards the coast on a farm track.

5. Roughly halfway down the slope, as the track snakes to the left, look out for a **waymarker post** with a yellow arrow on the right. A narrow but well-used path angles steeply downhill across the contours.

Roughly halfway down the slope, pause to look down at the village. In a small field behind houses is a flat-topped earthen mound, all that remains of a medieval motte and bailey castle. Known locally as

Llewelyn's Mound, or *Y Mŵd, it may once have been the court, or llys, of the Welsh prince, Llywelyn ap Iorwerth.*

At the foot of the slope, the path emerges onto a lane above **Abergwyngregyn**. Turn left to reach the family-run **Caffi Hen Felin** in the centre of the village, or right, uphill along the lane to return to the car parks at **Bont Newydd** to complete the walk. ♦

Aber Falls, or *Rhaeadr-fawr*

Formed by glacial action at the end of the last Ice Age, the Aber Falls, Rhaeadr-fawr (or 'great waterfall'), plummets 120 feet/37 metres over an igneous sill into the plunge pool below. It's one of the highest waterfalls in Wales and at its most spectacular after prolonged or heavy rain, or when frozen solid in winter. At full force, the Aber Falls' thundering water and curtains of spray can be truly awe-inspiring.

The Erskine Arms in the centre of Conwy

The **Erskine Arms**, Conwy

A fascinating walk around part of the medieval town walls, with a bracing hill and coast walk to finish

What to expect:
*Good hill and coast paths; one **very steep** descent. Good footwear required*

Distance/time: 8 kilometres/ 5 miles. Allow 2 – 2½ hours

Start: Conwy town car park outside the town walls in Llanrwst Road (OR Morfa Conwy beach car park SH 761 786)

Grid ref: SH 781 773

Ordnance Survey map: OS Explorer OL17 Snowdon/Yr Wyddfa - *Conwy Valley/Dyffryn Conwy*

The Pub: The Erskine Arms, Rose Hill Street, Conwy LL32 8DL | 01492 593535 | www.erskinearms.co.uk

Walk outline: Beginning in the shadow of Conwy's famous castle, a climb onto the medieval town walls leads through the upper town and onto the lower slopes of Conwy Mountain with its stunning coastal views. A steep descent and a short road section take you out to the coast with a bracing walk along the dunes of Morfa Conwy, before turning into the conwy estuary and a return to Conwy.

The Erskine Arms is an interesting mix of Georgian coaching inn and 17th century sail-maker's cottage and has been beautifully renovated to produce a warm, inviting pub arranged on split levels. Local ales and excellent food make this the perfect end to a lovely coastal walk.

Britain's smallest house

▶ The Erskine Arms at a glance

Open: Mon to Sat 11.30am – 11pm | Sun 11.30pm – 10.30pm

Brewery/company: Stange & Co Pubs

Ales and wine: Selection of local ales including Conwy, plus extensive wine list

Food: Daily 12pm – 9pm. Delicious menu of homemade pub classics along with seasonal specials. Selection of roasts served on Sundays.

Outside: Secluded courtyard perfect to trap the summer sun and to keep away the cooler autumn winds.

Children & dogs: Children's menu and highchairs available. Changing facilities available. Dogs are welcome in our bar area and in our courtyard.

The Walk

1. Head towards the **subway** at the back of the car park (leads under the railway and gives access to the town). Immediately before the subway, take the rising road on the left signed to **Tŵr Llewelyn**. The road leads up beside the railway and through an **archway** in the **town walls**. Turn right immediately and climb the **spiral stairway** up onto the walls.

The town walls are some of the best preserved medieval walls in Europe. They were built, along with the castle, by Edward I in 1283 following his conquest of Wales.

The walls can be walked for almost three quarters of their length. The first section is along a wooden walkway, then, after the first **corner tower**, the original stone walkway continues to the **Upper Gate**, where there is another **spiral stairway**. Descend the stairway, turn right through the walls and bear left along the road.

2. Ignore a left (St Agnes Road) continuing ahead. Take the fourth turning on the right into **Cadnant Park**. Follow the road, which soon descends gradually before swinging right. Immediately after this, turn left into 'Mountain Road'. Follow the road as it swings left, then rises. Ignoring a right, continue on the rising road and where it forks at the end of the tarmac, bear right up to a stile. Cross the stile and follow the clear footpath ahead onto **Conwy Mountain**.

The well worn path rises gradually through the trees. Shortly after you emerge from the woods, the path levels by a distinct flat rock. Turn right here and

"One of the most impressive walled circuits in Europe"

walk out to an impressive **viewpoint** overlooking Conwy and the river mouth.

The superb view from here takes in the wide sweep of Conwy Bay, from the east coast of Anglesey and Puffin Island to the Great Orme and Llandudno. You can see almost the entire route from here.

3. Turn around with your back to the estuary and bear right onto a grassy path. In about 50 metres turn right onto a narrow path that cuts diagonally down the steep slopes (**care needed**) towards the main road below. Partway down the slope, turn right again and head

more steeply down towards a stile visible below.

Cross the stile and the road opposite **'Bryn Morfa' caravan park** entrance and turn left along the road. Cross the **A55** and take the first left signed to **'Abercoanwy Resort & Spa'**.

Walk past the Spa entrance and immediately before the **beach car park** turn sharp right onto the coastal path. The path follows the top of the **sand dunes** between the **golf course** and the beach with views out over the river mouth to the Great Orme.

The amazing panorama across Afon Conwy to the Great Orme from Conwy Mountain

4. At the far end of the golf course, the dunes curve rightwards into the mouth of **Afon Conwy**. Pass through the car park and slipway and continue ahead on a footpath to reach **Conwy Quays Marina** on the right.

Turn right and follow the path beside the marina. Turn left along the path between the marina and the houses on the water front. Before you reach the far end, look for the signed **Wales Coast Path** directing you right between the houses. Take the left fork in a few metres keeping ahead to a road T junction (**Telford Close**). Turn left, then first right to cross over the A55.

In around 200 metres turn left immediately before the **school** onto a tarmaced footpath. This follows the edge of the estuary into Conwy.

5. At the end of the path turn left through the **town walls** and walk along the **waterfront** passing the famous **smallest house in Wales**.

Immediately after the **Liverpool Arms**, turn right through **Lower Gate** in the walls and walk up **High Street** keeping ahead at the crossroads.

You will pass Aberconwy House on the left and Plas Mawr on the right partway up High Street, both fine period houses.

6. At the top of the rise in the centre of the town, a left turn along **Church Street** will take you to the **Erskine Arms**.

Leave the Erskine Arms by the main entrance and turn left along **Rose Hill Street**. Cross the road after the **Visitor Centre**, take the path through the gatehouse and down the steps. Turn right through the subway to return to the car park to complete the walk. ♦

Plas Mawr

Plas Mawr, meaning the 'Great Hall', was built between 1576 and 1585 by Robert Wynn an influential and prosperous Welsh merchant. It is said to be the best preserved Elizabethan town house to be found anywhere in Britain. The house is noted for both the quality and quantity of ornamental plasterwork which proclaimed Wynn's status and wealth. Plas Mawr is held in the care of Cadw and open to the public. www.cadw.gov.wales

A calm morning at Llyn Crafnant

Llyn Crafnant

A picturesque walk linking two of the most popular lakes in the area: Crafnant and Geirionydd

What to expect:
Forest tracks and footpaths, uneven and sometimes muddy in places

Distance/time: 8 kilometres/ 5 miles. Allow 2½ hours

Start: Parking is available in a large Forestry Commission car park just before the lake. WC facilities are provided

Grid ref: SH 756 618

Ordnance Survey Map: Explorer OL17 *Snowdon/ Yr Wyddfa Conwy Valley/ Dyffryn Conwy*

After the walk: Pubs and tearooms in Trefriw.

Walk outline

From the car park, the route leads up to, then along the wooded edge of Llyn Crafnant to the head of the crag-lined valley. A short section along the quiet lane is followed by a gentle climb over the wooded ridge with more lakeside walking above the shore of Llyn Geirionydd. A return to the car park is made on forest paths and tracks.

Llyn Crafnant and Llyn Geirionydd

Llyn Crafnant and Llyn Geirionydd lie within the extensive plantations of the Gwydir Forest on the edge of the Carneddau mountains. Surrounded by woods and enclosed by the sheltering ridges of Creigiau Gleision and the shapely Crimpiau, these two lakes provide a quiet peaceful focus for this beautiful walk.

Crafnant takes its name from '*craf*', an old Welsh word for garlic and '*nant*', a stream or valley. Geirionydd has literary links to both ancient bards and more recent Eisteddfodau of the nineteenth century.

Wild garlic and bluebells are still a feature of these woods in the Spring months .

Bluebells above Llyn Crafnant

Wild garlic

The Walk

1. Take the yellow waymarked route out of the car park and turn right along the lane. Walk up the lane to **Llyn Crafnant**.

This will be your first view of Llyn Crafnant and the beautiful valley that encloses it. The name Crafnant is possibly derived from the words 'craf'—which refers to garlic and 'nant'—a valley or stream. If this is the case, the name Crafnant means: 'stream' or 'valley of garlic'.

A column near the outflow of the lake records the gift made by Richard James of Dyffryn Aur to Llanrwst Parish Council in 1895, enabling them to take a water supply from the lake.

Turn right immediately before the lake, pass through a kissing gate, and follow a **forest road** above the lake shore. Keep left at a fork in the track, about half way along the lake.

At the head of the lake, the track becomes narrows to a footpath. The path passes between some **large boulders** and through kissing gates before swinging left to cross a **footbridge** over the stream to join the access track to '**Hendre**', on the right. Turn left along the track and follow it to a tarmac lane. Turn left along the lane for almost 1 kilometre/½ mile.

2. Immediately after a bridge over the stream and opposite a **small stone**

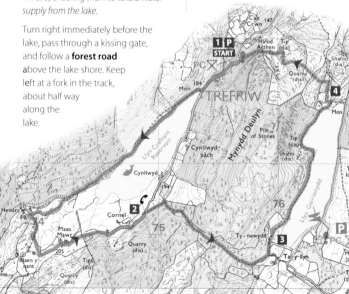

An atmospheric woodland path between the two lakes

cottage, bear right off the lane onto a footpath. Rise steadily to meet a path junction and turn right. Follow the well-worn footpath up through woods.

At the top of the rise, go through a **gap in the wall** and a short drop brings you to a forestry road. Follow the road down the hill and in about 50 metres keep right where the forest road forks and almost immediately, turn left onto a **narrow footpath**. This path heads directly downhill crossing the forest road twice before you arrive at a T junction with fields below and ahead. Turn left

along the track and where the this bends right, bear left over a stile below a **cottage**.

3. Walk through the following field with the waters of **Llyn Geirionydd** to the right. Enter the woods and continue along the water's edge for about ¾ mile. (The first section of path along the shore of the lake is poor in places, so most walkers bear left up to a forest track just before the stile out of the field and follow this above the lake shore.)

As you approach the end of the lake, leave the woods behind and follow the

A faint morning mist on the mirror calm Llyn Crafnant

footpath ahead to a **small stone barn** on the right. Immediately after this, turn left along the access road to a house and after 20 metres or so, turn right and walk up to a **stone monument**. This gives a fine view of Llyn Geirionydd and the steep wooded hillside of Mynydd Deulyn.

The monument commemorates Taliesin, a famous sixth century bard (see box opposite) and is also noted for its associations with the Eisteddfod organised by the bard Gwilym Cowlyd (real name William John Roberts), in the second half of the nineteenth century. He worked as a poet, printer and bookseller and published

the works of a number of fellow poets. As a bard he was highly respected and won the Chair at the National Eisteddfod at Conwy in 1861. His high standards led him into disagreement with the rules, however, so together with an associate, he organised a rival Eisteddfod in 1863 under the name of 'Arwest Glan Geirionydd'. The location was here around the Taliesin monument for obvious reasons and for a while it rivalled the National Eisteddfod in popularity, attracting entries from all over Wales.

4. Drop to a path directly behind the monument, bear right and keep to the right of a small group of conifers.

Beyond the trees follow the path down to cross a **stone wall** by a stile. Immediately after the stile, keep ahead at a fork and follow a rising path through young birch woods. After a second wall at a T junction a little further on, turn left.

Stay on the clear path eventually passing through an area of **old mines**. A stile now leads onto a forestry road. Keep right at a fork down the hill to return to the car park and complete the walk. ♦

Taliesin Monument

On a hillside overlooking the northern end of Llyn Geirionydd is a monument to one of the earliest poets in the Welsh language. Taliesin Ben Beirdd — or 'Taliesin, Chief of Bards' — was a celebrated royal poet who served at least three Welsh kings. The Book of Taliesin is a later, tenth century, manuscript containing his poems. Taliesin lived on the shores of Llyn Geirionydd long ago, and is said by some to be buried here too.

The peaks of the Snowdon Horseshoe from Llynnau Mymbyr

SPECTACULAR VIEWPOINT

Capel Curig

A straight forward walk with the constant backdrop of Snowdonia's most iconic mountain panorama

What to expect:
Good paths through pasture, woods and riverside; spectacular views

Distance/time: 7 kilometres/ 4¼ miles. Allow 2½ hours

Start: Begin the walk from the car park situated behind the shops in Capel Curig

Grid ref: SH 720 581

Ordnance Survey Map: Explorer OL17 *Snowdon/ Yr Wyddfa Conwy Valley/ Dyffryn Conwy*

After the walk: Pubs and cafe in Capel Curig

Walk outline

Starting in Capel Curig, the route leads up to the little rocky summit know as Capel Curig Pinnacles, well known for its stunning view of Snowdon, before continuing on to the watershed between Capel Curig and the Crafnant valley. On the high saddle you are treated to a commanding view of the entire valley with Snowdon as the centre piece, before a gentle descent. Return is made by a riverside path ending at Llynnau Mymbyr for the the most famous view in Snowdonia. Save this walk for good, clear weather to fully appreciate the views.

The view

There are few mountain views, even amongst the dramatic scenery of Snowdonia (and possibly even the UK), to rival the prospect of the four summits of the Snowdon Horseshoe viewed across the placid waters of Llynnau Mymbyr at Capel Curig. The composition is ready made and artists and photographers have marvelled at this view for centuries.

Keep your eye open for peregrines and buzzards over the higher ground, along with the occasional red kite. They can be identified by their distinctive forked tail.

Milestone near Capel Curig

Red kite

The Walk

1. Turn left out of the car park and walk over the **old bridge** to join the road with shops to your left. Turn half-left, cross the **A5** and take the signed footpath directly opposite beside the **war memorial**. This rises through grazing fields towards the small rocky peak which overlooks Capel Curig (**Capel Curig Pinnacles**) and gives a classic view of the Snowdon group rising beyond Llynnau Mymbyr. *It is worth the short detour off the path to the top of the pinnacles for this classic view.*

2. The path passes to the left of the rocks, eventually entering woods by a stile or gate. Follow the clear footpath ahead through the trees, then across the bracken covered hillside below **Clogwyn Mawr**. Climb the ladder stile and continue ahead on the pitched path.

Just before the wooden footbridge, turn sharp right beside the stream to cross a small **stone footbridge**. Cross a second smaller **footbridge**, pass a gate on your left and keep beside a **garden** to cross a ladder stile lower down. Turn

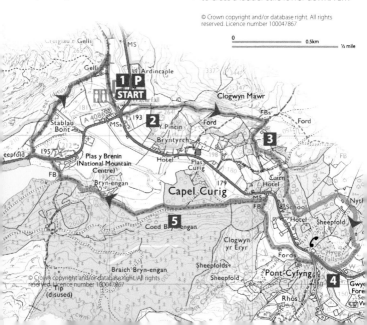

The Snowdon Horseshoe dominates the view from Capel Curig Pinnacles

left by the fence and left again to reach a rough access track beside the gate to **Bryn Tyrch Uchaf**. Turn left along the access track for a few metres, then bear left again onto a path beside the fence on your left.

3. Pass above an attractive **wooden house** in a superb setting, to reach a ladder stile. Cross the stile and go ahead through the gap in a wall of large boulders. Head aross a small field and walk down to cross a stile into **woods**. Follow the clear footpath down through the trees.

At a fork, bear left onto a contouring path and continue through the woods. Pass a small **stone building** on the left and, a little further on, meet a rising track at a T junction. Turn left up the hill and after passing through a gap in a stone wall look for an obvious path on the right. Follow this path with good views both into and along the valley and across to Moel Siabod.

Continue to a T junction with a footpath near a small **cottage** on the left. Turn right down the hill to a stile which leads to a car park by **Bryn Glo café**.

The peaks of the Snowdon Horseshoe from Llynnau Mymbyr

4. Turn right along the main road (**A5**). Shortly, turn left over the **old stone bridge** and take the signed footpath on the right almost immediately, which follows an access road for a few metres before bearing right down the bank after a cattle grid.

Cross the **footbridge** and go ahead across a field to the **river**. Bear left now and walk beside the river.

In the corner of the last field, a ladder stile takes you into **woods**. Follow the riverside footpath ahead until you reach a **footbridge** on the right. Don't cross the footbridge, stay on the rising path

ahead and at the top of the rise turn right through 'slits' in the rock. Follow a footpath beside the fence with the river and the A5 down to your right.

5. Continue on the good forest path to a T junction with a forest road. Turn left here, then bear right shortly at a fork and follow the forest road to '**Bryn Engan**', a large house on the right.

Go through the gate straight ahead and continue on the forest road to the footbridge at **Plas-y-Brenin** (meaning 'King's Palace' or 'Hall') **Outdoor Education Centre**.

Turn right over the **footbridge**.

The view to the Snowdon group from the shore of Llynnau Mymbyr here is perhaps the most famous view in the whole of Snowdonia and it is easy to see why.

Rise to the road, turn left and after 150 metres or so, turn right over a ladder stile. The path curves right to contour the hillside (ignore a farm track on the right). Continue to join a rough farm road after a cottage on the right. Turn right here and return to Capel Curig to complete the walk. ♦

Plas y Brenin

Plas-y-Brenin is now a well established outdoor pursuits centre but was originally built as a sixty-room hotel during the first decade of the nineteenth century when it was known as 'The Royal Hotel'. It was built by Lord Penrhyn who owned the Penrhyn slate quarries at Bethesda and who was responsible for building the first coach road through the Ogwen Valley between 1791 and 1800, where previously there had only been a packhorse trail.

Leaving the shelter of the dunes at Harlech for the open beach

Harlech beach

A moderate walk with stunning views, a stretch of beach and a historic castle and town

What to expect:
Farmland paths, quiet lanes, beach and town roads

Distance/time: 7 kilometres/ 4½ miles. Allow 2–2½ hours

Start: Bron-y-Graig Uchaf long stay Pay & Display car park in the centre of Harlech. Short stay is next to the road, long stay around the corner

Grid ref: SH 582 309

Ordnance Survey Map: OS Explorer OL 18 Snowdonia *Harlech, Porthmadog & Y Bala*

After the walk: Cafés, restaurants and pubs in Harlech

Walk outline

Climbing to the lush farmland above the town of Harlech gives tremendous views across the Bay. On a clear day you can see the long arm of the Llŷn Peninsula reaching out into the Irish Sea. The walk then drops down through the quiet village of Llanfair, before snaking down steep steps near the cliffs to join the beach for almost a mile. The walk returns to Harlech with a steep climb to the castle and the town.

Harlech

Harlech is a quiet town dominated by the dark and brooding castle that sits handsomely on its rock, keeping watch over Tremadog Bay. It is one of Edward I's iron ring of castles, built along the coast of Wales in the 13th century to subdue the Welsh. Harlech was also the headquarters of Owain Glyndŵr during his rebellion in the 15th century.

Many of Harlech's visitors come for the wide sandy beach and historic castle, but there are hidden gems to be found on the rolling hills behind the town. These gentle pastures give some of the best views in the area.

Castle from the dunes

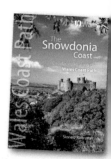

More coastal walks ...

It's easy to find your own space on one of the largest beaches in Wales

The Walk

1. Leave the car park and turn right along the road. At the next junction, turn left, uphill.

At the end of the road by metal posts go straight up and soon bear left for a signed grassy path. At the top of the path reach a rough track: turn right as waymarked (on the wall ahead) and then very soon turn left at a 'Public Footpath' sign along the road. Shortly, bear left again alongside the wall of a house to find a narrow footpath rising up ahead.

2. Follow this grassy track to some **gates**. Go through the first wooden gate and almost immediately turn left to go through a large metal gate by the waymarker on the post that points right up the grassy field.

Follow the waymarkers across the field, through gaps in two low **stone walls**.

It's worth pausing to turn around here and appreciate the fine and far-reaching views across the bay. If visibility is good, look for the tip of Bardsey Island at the end of the Llŷn Peninsula on the far left. The towns of Criccieth and Porthmadog are directly ahead with Snowdon sitting behind them a little further to the right. The Moelwyns and Cnicht are the mountains on the far right.

Continue ahead to a stile in a **stone wall**. Cross it and follow the obvious path through the field to a gap in another stone wall. Go through the gap and continue with the wall to your right. At the top of the field, bear right through another gap and then left to join a **green lane** flanked by walls.

At the end of the lane is an open field. Turn right and follow the stone wall beneath **power lines**. As the wall veers right, ignore a gap but stay ahead to aim for some houses and eventually reach a stile over the wall.

Don't cross this stile, but instead turn left and walk alongside the wall to reach a gate onto a lane.

3. Turn right along the lane, then, almost immediately, bear left at a 'Public Footpath' sign by a **cattle grid**. Over the grid, bear immediately right onto a grassy path leading to a small gate into a field.

Bear right, to cross the field diagonally, passing some stone piles and an **electricity pole** on the left, heading towards the field corner, then look right for a stone stile over the wall.

Cross it and head straight down this field through a gateway and onto a grassy track. Continue ahead again

0 _____ 1km
_____ ½ mile

Dark rain clouds gather over Harlech beach and dunes

down the field, staying quite close to the wall on the right and you'll soon see a wall beginning on the left. There's a path (sometimes overgrown and muddy) between these two walls so follow this straight down to a gate onto a lane.

4. At the lane turn right, then at the crossroads go straight over, passing a bus stop. At the next junction, turn right along the pavement until you see a coast path waymarker and **National Trust sign** opposite.

5. Cross the road and go through the gate then follow the path down **Harlech Cliffs** as it zig-zags to some

steps to the **railway line**. Cross the line, go down to the beach and turn right.

6. Walk along **Harlech beach** for just over 1.5 kilometres/1 mile.

At the main entrance, turn right to follow the sandy path to a tarmac track. Go through the gate and pass a **car park** on the left.

Continue ahead along the lane past the **school** and at the end turn right. Cross the railway line, then very soon cross the road and bear left for a lane signed for the 'Town Centre'.

7. Follow this as it zig-zags steeply uphill, eventually passing **Harlech Castle** on

the left. Continue, to reach a junction with the **High Street** and turn right.

Walk along the High Street, then after a pretty **cobbled square** turn left up a steep footpath which leads past **St Tanwg's Church** and back to the car park to complete the walk. ♦

Harlech Castle

Harlech is one of Edward I's finest Welsh castles. It took a thousand men seven years to build and was completed in 1290. It was attacked almost immediately by Welsh freedom fighters. Captured by Owain Glyndwr in the fifteenth century, it became his home and headquarters for four years before being retaken by the English Prince Henry. Today, Harlech Castle is a designated UNESCO World Heritage Site cared for by Cadw.

Looking down to Llyn Idwal from below the Devil's Kitchen

walk 6

Llyn Idwal & Llyn Ogwen

A circuit of two of the most famous and dramatic mountain lakes in Snowdonia

What to expect:

Rough and rocky mountain paths, boggy in places. Waterproof walking boots required

Distance/time: 9 kilometres/ 5½ miles. Allow 2½ – 3½ hours

Start: Free parking in the large layby on the A5 at the eastern end of Llyn Ogwen

Grid ref: SH 668 605

Ordnance Survey Map: OS Explorer OL17 Snowdon/Yr Wyddfa – *Conwy Valley/Dyffryn Conwy*

After the walk: Snack bar at Ogwen Cottage, pub and café in Capel Curig (4 miles east) 01248 689454

Walk outline

Starting below the rugged rock peak of Tryfan, a rough, uneven path takes you along the northern shore of Llyn Ogwen with widening views. At Ogwen Cottage there are public toilets and a snack bar. The route then heads up into the spectacular mountain hollow of Cwm Idwal below the famous Devil's Kitchen, for a circuit of Llyn Idwal with impressive views. You will be able to ponder the amazing discovery of Charles Darwin who after studying this valley realised that much of our mountain landscape was carved by ancient glaciers. After a circuit of the lake a return is made to Ogwen.

The Idwal Slabs

Llyn Ogwen & Llyn Idwal

These are two of the most famous lakes in Snowdonia. Often described as 'ribbon lakes' from their shared glacial origins, their circuit presents walkers with spectacular views of the Glyderau and Carneddau mountains, including the unique rock preak of Tryfan and the rugged mountain amphitheatre of Cwm Idwal. The walk will also give you a close up view of the huge rock cleft known as 'The Devil's Kitchen. Lookout for the feral goats that can often be seen on the upper slopes above Llyn Idwal.

Feral goat

The Walk

1. From the layby cross the road and take the access track over the **river** by the **stone bridge** and pass through a small group of **pines**. Pass 'Glan Denna' on the left and continue over the cattle grid on the farm track.

Just before the **farm** turn right onto the signed path up beside the **wall**. At a stile on the left, cross the wall. Don't take the path that bends right up beside the stream here, instead, bear left in a few metres on a less distinct path heading towards the **lake**. Pass

above the farm and cross the stream by two **footbridges**. From here the path continues ahead on a contouring line with Llyn Ogwen down to your left. This path is waymarked for the '**Snowdonia Slate Trail**' by white topped posts.

This path gives excellent views of Tryfan, the Glyderau, Y Garn and the Devil's Kitchen rising above Cwm Idwal at the end of the lake. These shady north facing cwms are the result of small hanging glaciers which lingered on the northern slopes of the mountains during periods of time when the climate was much colder. The result is the dramatic contrast between the craggy northeastern and the more gentle southwestern slopes of all the mountains in Britain.

The path, a little vague at first, keeps directly ahead not straying too far from a line of **overhead cables**.

A little over halfway along the lake, the path gradually drops to eventually run close to the shore of the lake.

A fleeting rainbow over Llyn Ogwen

2. Near the end of the lake, make your way through an area of **huge boulders** to the reach the **road (A5)**. Turn left and walk along the road to **Ogwen Cottage**.

Turn right along the access road to the car park and immediately before the **snack bar** and **toilets**, turn left onto the **Llyn Idwal path**. Within a few metres the path forks—take a right here (Idwal path continues ahead) and follow the path through a **small rock gorge**.

A pitched path leads out of the gorge on the right and heads across open, and sometimes boggy ground, towards the Devil's Kitchen. At an area of **smooth flat rocks** you get a brief view down into Nant Ffrancon to the right. Cross a stile over the fence and a little further on turn left at a fork and walk down to the shore of **Llyn Idwal**.

The rocks of the cwm are mainly volcanic, thought to be 450 million years old and are distorted into a huge 'U' shaped fold — known as the 'Idwal Syncline' — which can be seen in rock layers forming the distinctive terraces on either side of the Devil's Kitchen. The present form of the cwm however, owes its existence to much more recent events—the action of ice

The spectacular amphitheatre of Cwm Idwal

during the last Ice Age. Evidence suggests that at its greatest extent ice spilled over from above the Devil's Kitchen and flowed down into the cwm in the form of an ice tongue up to 1,500 feet thick which then joined the main Ogwen/Nant Ffrancon glacier. As the ice dwindled it left behind the mounds of debris known as 'moraines' which can be seen around the path on the north side of the lake.

Turn right along the shore and go through the **kissing gate** in the **wall**. The path leads above the shore of the lake, soon passing through a series of mounds. These are the **moraine ridges** mentioned previously.

3. At the head of the lake there is a prominent path junction. Turn left and follow the pitched path towards the huge face formed by the **Idwal Slabs**.

4. At the T junction turn left onto the well-worn lakeside path. At the outflow turn around for a final view of the lake before taking the pitched path back towards Ogwen Cottage.

There are a couple of options now:
The easiest and most straightforward is to return to Ogwen Cottage and head back along the A5 — about 1¼ miles of walking along the road.

Alternatively, a more interesting but more challenging route is to turn right

where the path makes a prominent left
turn. Follow the path until just before
begins to climb steeply beside the
cascading stream. Head left here across
open boggy ground heading for the
high-hand end of Llyn Ogwen which

should soon be visible. Join a path
which leads down to one of the car
parks about halfway along the lake. Turn
right along the road to complete the
walk. ♦

Earth's frozen past discovered

*It was here in Cwm Idwal that the glacial origin of our
highland landscape was first discovered. This incredible
insight was made by Charles Darwin, best known for his
theories on evolution. In 1842 he came here following his
famous voyage on 'The Beagle' to South America and
was stuck by the similarities with the glacial landscaes
he had observed there. "A house burnt down by fire did
not tell it's story more plainly than did this valley."*

Mynydd Mawr and Foel Rudd rising above Llyn Cwellyn

Mynydd Mawr

An excellent mini mountain walk with grand views into Nantlle and across to the famous Nantlle Ridge

What to expect:
Good forest tracks, grassy paths on the higher slopes and a rocky descent

Distance/time: 10.5 kilometres/ 6½ miles. Allow 3½ – 4½ hours

Start: Begin in the village of Rhyd-Ddu on the A4085 Caernarfon to Beddgelert road. There are paying car parks for Snowdon immediately south of the village

Grid ref: SH 569 530

Ordnance Survey Map: OS Explorer OL17 Snowdon/Yr Wyddfa – *Conwy Valley/Dyffryn Conwy*

After the walk: Pub at Rhyd-Ddu

Walk outline
Easy walking on forest tracks to access a sweeping grassy ridge which is followed to the sub-summit of Foel Rudd and finally Mynydd Mawr. Views into Nantlle across the crags of Craig y Bera are magnificent. Descent is made by Afon Gôch, rocky in its lower section, to the shores of Llyn Cwellyn, with a lakeside return along forest tracks.

Mynydd Mawr
Mynydd Mawr is one of those hills that suffers from its close proximity to Snowdon. Standing barely chest high to its giant neighbour, the vast majority of visitors turn their backs on it and head in the opposite direction. But this great little hill is certainly not without interest. It has an impressive craggy southern face rising above Dyffryn Nantlle, a huge castle-like north face rearing up above Llyn Cwellyn, narrow grassy ridges and the hidden valley of Cwm Planwydd. All are visited on this lovely route starting in the village of Rhyd-Ddu.

Keep an eye open for the formidable peregrine, which nest on Mynydd Mawr's high, inaccessible crags.

Mynydd Mawr summit

More hill walks and easy summits ...

The Walk

1. From the 'Cwellyn Arms' in the centre of **Rhyd-Ddu** (junction of the A4085 and B4418) take the **B4418 Nantlle road**. In about 150 metres, turn right onto a forest road immediately after 'Cefn Cwellyn'. Follow the forest road for just over 1km/¾ mile before bearing left on a signed footpath that climbs to a stile on the edge of the woods.

2. Cross the stile and turn right along the forest edge following the crest of the ridge. At the end of the trees, climb the steepening grassy ridge ahead to

gain the subsidiary **summit of Foel Rudd**.

Follow the easy-angled connecting ridge westwards from **Foel Rudd** passing along the crest of **Craig y Bera** with dramatic views down the shattered crags to the pastures of Nantlle below.

Soon the path veers right-wards away from the cliffs to make an easy rise to the rounded summit of **Mynydd Mawr** with its superb views to Snowdon and south to the famous Nantlle Ridge.

3. Return can be made via the ascent route, but a more interesting circular walk with more of an exploratory feel can be made by returning to the crest of **Craig y Bera**, then bearing left down easy angled, but initially pathless heather slopes, with occasional scree, to join a faint path on the left bank of **Afon Gôch**.

Lower down, just before the angle steepens and you can see **Llyn Cwellyn** below, cross over to the right bank of the stream. This avoids difficult ground where the stream cascades into a small **ravine**

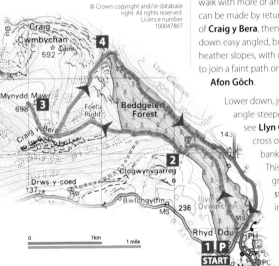

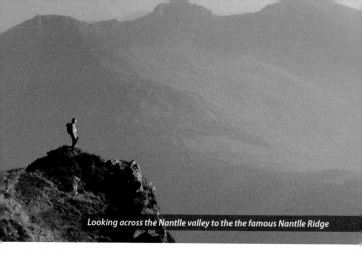

Looking across the Nantlle valley to the the famous Nantlle Ridge

beneath the dark dripping crags of **Castell Cidwm** *('Castle of the Wolf')*.

4. Below the ravine and waterfall, and just before woods, cross the stream again. Make your way between rocks and young pines to cross a stone wall in the corner by a **rock face** on the left. Walk down to the shore of **Llyn Cwellyn**.

Just before the water turn right on a path to a gate that continues to pass a small **quarry** on the right. Soon, join a forest track and follow it to the road (A4085). Turn right and follow the road back to Rhyd-Ddu to complete the walk. ♦

Mountain or hill?

The name Mynydd Mawr translates as 'great' or 'big mountain', yet its modest height suggests a hill rather than a mountain. In this case the 'great' or big' refers to the bulky nature of Mynydd Mawr rather than its height. Another name for this hill was 'Elephant Mountain' — again a reference to its bulky form rather than its height.

Looking to the high Carneddau from Tal y Fan

Tal y Fan

A fairly easy walk along a broad ridge with superb views of mountain and coast

What to expect:

Good footpaths over heather moors and grassy fields. Rocky in places on the ridge

Distance/time: 8 kilometres/ 5 miles. Allow 2½ – 3½ hours

Start: Drive through the village of Rowen and continue up the narrow lane for 1¾ miles to a T junction. Turn right and just after the lane swings left there is room for one or two cars on the verge

Grid ref: SH 731 715

Ordnance Survey Map: OS Explorer OL17 Snowdon/Yr Wyddfa – *Conwy Valley/Dyffryn Conwy*

After the walk: Pub in Rowen

Walk outline

A steady walk from a high start point to gain the heathery, rounded Tal y Fan ridge where an out-and-back path takes you to summit of Foel Lwyd. The jaunt along the ridge to Tal y Fan summit is a delight in good weather with magnificent views across eastern Anglesey and along the coast to the Great Orme and beyond. A steep, grassy descent, followed by a good contouring path completes the round.

Tal y Fan

The name Tal y Fan means the 'place at the end', and describes it perfectly. This little hill is the northern-most summit in the Carneddau range, the 'place', at the 'end' of the mountains. Though modest in height, Tal y Fan is a prominent feature in views looking west across the northern Conwy Valley and you will be able to enjoy unrivalled views all the way along the ridge.

This northern edge of Snowdonia is littered with prehistoric remains. The walk passes a Bronze Age standing stone known as Maen Penddu and you will probably see several semi-wild Welsh mountain ponies that thrive on these open slopes.

Maen Penddu standing stone

More hill walks and easy summits ...

The Walk

1. Walk back along the tarmac lane (the distance will depend on where you parked) to reach the **signed footpath** over the **wall** on the north side of the lane. A good path rises directly up through two rough grazing fields separated by a stone wall and crossed by a stile.

Just below the crest of the ridge, cross a **stile over the wall** on the right. Turn left up beside the wall at first, then veer half-right to the rounded crest of the ridge where another stile leads over the wall. Cross the stile.

2. To include **Foel Lwyd** (worth it for the views of the Carneddau) turn left along the broad ridge and follow the path

beside the wall. Return to this point to continue.

For **Tal y Fan** turn right (ahead from Foel Lwyd) and follow the path along the ridge — a mix of grass, heather and rocks — with wide views on both sides.

The summit is marked by a triangulation pillar on the far side of the fence. Views take in eastern Anglesey, the Great Orme and northern Carneddau.

Continue to the eastern end of the ridge and, where the **wall** turns to the right and begins to drop, bear left down the northern slopes. Take one of the faint paths which drop into a small hollow

Tal y Fan offers superb views over to Anglesey and along the coast to Llandudno

where there is a **small stone enclosure** on the left. Continue ahead and soon you will be able to see to a small **fenced area of mine workings** below. Pass the mines on their left-hand side to join an obvious track immediately below the spoil heap. Follow this track to a T junction with another track and turn right.

3. Shortly you pass a small Bronze Age standing stone, **Mean Penddu,** on the right. About 15 metres beyond the stone, and just before the track bends left, bear half-right off the track and aim for a large **metal gate** in the wall ahead. About 10-15 metres before the gate, bear left to walk beside a stream and soon you will pick up a reasonable path between stone walls. Stay by the left-hand wall until it opens out into a large field. Walk straight ahead through the centre of the field in the direction of a small pointed rocky summit ahead. In the bottom corner, go through a **gap in the wall** and walk ahead to eventually meet a grass track. Turn right along the track.

4. Follow the track, ignoring a left fork, soon with a ruined wall on the left. The path curves right beside a well-built wall and continues ahead. After a gate in a crossing wall the path continues ahead.

Eventually a **cottage (Cae Coch)** comes into view ahead. The path passes below the cottage and curves left to reach a **farm track**. Turn right along the track to reach the tarmac lane. Go ahead along the lane to complete the walk. ♦

Craig Cau dominates the dark Llyn Cau

Cadair Idris

A tough and spectacular mountain walk with grand views comparable with an ascent of Snowdon

What to expect:

Steep, rough mountain paths; over high mountain terrain. Some exposure

---

Distance/time: 9.5 kilometres/ 6 miles. Allow 5 – 6 hours

Start: The National Park car park at Dôl Idris, located just off the junction of the A487 and the B4405l

Grid ref: SH 732 115

Ordnance Survey Map: Ordnance Survey Outdoor Leisure OL32 *Cadair Idris & Llyn Tegid*

Walk outline

Steep walking on a good path through a wooded gorge leads to the impressive mountain lake of Llyn Cau enclosed by the dark crags of Craig Cau. A fine ridge walk leads over Mynydd Pencoed and on to Cadair's highest point — Penygadair. Easy walking along the summit plateau to the subsidiary summit of Mynydd Moel, followed by a steep descent over rounded slopes to rejoin the outward route in the wooded gorge.

Cadair Idris

There is little doubt that the most memorable view of Cadair Idris is from the north, either across the broad sand flats of the Mawddach estuary, or the calm waters of Llynnau Cregennen below the northern cliffs of Tyrrau Mawr. From the south the mountain is rather featureless and has far less impact, but concealed in these softer folds is the most impressive mountain cwm south of Snowdon.

Views to Cardigan Bay

This route follows the classic round of Cwm Cau, a superb ridge walk in spectacular surroundings and undoubtedly the best route on the mountain. The red kite is an increasingly common sight in Southern Snowdonia, identifiable by its distinctive 'forked' tail.

More mountain walks ...

The Walk

1. Go through the gate at the back of the car park by the information board and turn right along an **avenue of trees**. Cross the bridge and soon pass in front of the 'Ystradlyn Visitor Centre'. After the footbridge, turn right through a gate into the **nature reserve** to begin

the stiff pull up through woods beside the tumbling **Nant Cadair** stream over to the right.

2. As you emerge from the woods the path soon bends left towards the enclosed lake of **Llyn Cau** which remains out of view until you are almost at the water's edge.

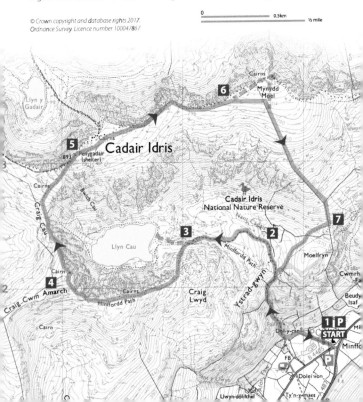

Grand views across Cyfrwy and Tyrrau Mawr to Cardigan Bay

Like the high valleys in northern Snowdonia, this mountain hollow is a textbook example of a glacial valley, carved by a small 'Alpine' glacier up to 250 metres thick. Classic features are the steep, near vertical headwall and valley sides, along with the deep lake gouged by the rotating action of the ice.

3. On the lip of the cwm the path splits — the path ahead leads down to the shore of the lake with the path to the left rising up towards the ridge.

It is worth the short detour to the edge of the lake for the stunning view of Craig Cau towering above the dark water, but you will need to return to this junction and take the left fork to continue.

As you gain the ridge you are treated to fine views southwards across to the Tarren hills and beyond. Follow the path along the edge of **Craig Cau** to the subsidiary top of **Mynydd Pencoed** perched on the very edge of the huge cliffs overhanging the lake (take care in poor visibility!).

4. From Mynydd Pencoed make a short descent due north to the saddle separating Craig Cau from Penygadair.

Llyn y Gadair nestles in the glacial hollow below Cadair Idris's north face

From here a short, stiff pull takes you onto the summit slopes and finally **Penygadair**, Cadair's highest point.

In clear conditions the view out over the Mawddach estuary and across Cardigan Bay to the distant hills of the Lleyn Peninsula is magnificent, particularly late in the day with the promise of a fine sunset. With reasonable clarity the entire curve of Cardigan Bay should be visible from Bardsey (Ynys Enlli) to the tip of Pembrokeshire.

The small ruined shelter on the summit is said to have once been used to offer refreshments to those making the ascent on pony from Tŷ Nant.

5. From the **summit**, head east across the broad summit plateau towards **Mynydd Moel**, just over 1 kilometre/¾ mile away.

6. As the ground begins the gentle rise to Mynydd Moel, either continue to the summit, or, if you want to miss out this minor top, take the contouring path that breaks away to the right. Eventually a **wall** is either reached or is visible down to the right. Head for this and descend steeply on its left-hand side.

Alternatively, from the summit of Mynydd Moel reach the wall by a direct descent south-southeast.

7. Follow the wall to a stile (in about 1

kilometre/¾ mile) on the right. Cross the wall here and head down rightwards to cross the stream (**Nant Cadair**) by a **footbridge** near the point where the Minffordd Path (used earlier) emerges from the woods.

Turn left here and retrace the outward route down through the woods beside the stream and Ystradlyn Visitor Centre to complete the walk . ♦

The 'Chair of Idris'

Cadair Idris means 'Chair of Idris', Idris being a personal name. The most likely candidate is Idris ap Gwyddno a prince of Meirionydd who won a battle on the mountain. Irdis was also known as 'Idris Gawr' — the Great or 'Giant'. This could be the origin of the legend that claims Cadair Idris to be the 'chair of the giant Idris. Chair in this context could also be taken as referring to the 'seat' or 'stronghold of Idris'.

Crib Goch rises above Bwlch Moch with Snowdon beyond

Snowdon/Yr Wyddfa

A grand mountain walk to the roof of Wales with interest and spectacular views every step of the way

What to expect:

Steep, rough mountain paths; over high mountain terrain. Seasonal summit cafe

Distance/time: 12 kilometres/ 7½ miles. Allow 5 – 7 hours

Start: There is a moderate sized car park at Pen-y-Pass (usually full). Alternatives at Pen-y-Gwyryd or Nant Peris Park & Ride. Fees payable

Grid ref: Pen-y-Pass SH 647 557; Peny-y-Gwyryd SH 659 557; Nant Peris Park & Ride SH 607 583

Ordnance Survey Map: OS Explorer OL17 Snowdon/Yr Wyddfa – Conwy Valley/Dyffryn Conwy

Walk outline

A gradual climb along a rocky, well constructed path leads to Bwlch Moch. From here you enter the Snowdon Horseshoe with its grand scenery. Old mine workings add extra interest, before the final climb up the famous 'Zig-zags' to join the Snowdon Mountain Railway and the Llanberis Path, which is followed to the summit. Descent is by a return down the 'Zig-zags' and a steep rocky path to Glaslyn and Llyn Llydaw. The remains of an old mining road are used to return to Pen-y-Pass.

Snowdon/Yr Wyddfa

From any approach Snowdon demands attention — its height, complexity and dramatic skylines dominate the whole of northern Snowdonia. Even the height and closeness of its neighbours takes nothing away from this great mountain. If you were to place it amongst the Munros of the Scottish Highlands it would have no shame.

As far as routes to the summit are concerned, you are spoilt for choice — but the most impressive of the classic paths are the routes from Pen-y-Pass which lead up through Cwm Dyli. Keep a look out for peregrines.

Bwlch Glas

More mountain walks ...

A cloud inversion creates stunning conditions on Snowdon's summit

The Walk

A path below the road links the parking area at Pen-y-Gwryd with Pen-y-pass.

1. From the **Pen-y-Pass** car park the obvious exit from the lower car park is the Miners' Track (return route). However the best ascent is via the **Pyg Track** which exits from the higher car park just behind the **café** ('Gorphwysfa Restaurant') through a **gap in the stone wall** and under power lines.

Follow the Pyg Track — a well constructed path with views down the Llanberis Pass and ahead to the shapely, pyramidal summit of Crib Goch to **Bwlch Moch**, the saddle on the ridge and the point at which you enter the Snowdon Horseshoe (about 1.5 kilometres/1 mile).

From Bwlch Moch there are superb views down to Llyn Llydaw and its causeway, and beyond to the 300-metre face of Y Lliwedd. Ahead is Snowdon looking deceptively close. To the right here is the steep path leading up to Crib Goch, but the Pyg Track continues over the stiles ahead to contour along the mountain's southern slopes.

2. Following the Pyg Track you eventually reach a superb viewpoint where Glaslyn (lake) and the dramatic summit cone of Snowdon can be seen to perfection rising above the lake.

Continue on the contouring path to an even closer viewpoint directly above Glaslyn.

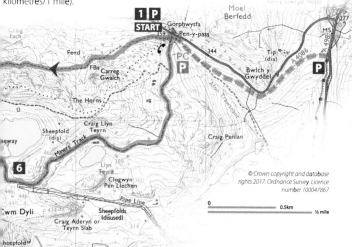

© Crown copyright and database rights 2017. Ordnance Survey. Licence number 100047867

The view from Bwlch Glas into Cwm Dyli with Snowdon on the right

3. From here the path curves around the cwm passing the **junction with the Miners' Track** which comes up from the left (marked by an upright stone — take note of this for the descent).

4. Higher up you reach the foot of the famous '**Zig-zags**' which negotiate the final steep slopes to **Bwlch Glas**.

The Bwlch Glas is marked by a **2-metre upright stone pillar** and it is here you meet with the Llanberis Path and the **Snowdon Mountain Railway**.

Turn left for the final ten-minute walk to the summit.

To descend, return to the upright stone on Bwlch Glas and descend the 'Zig-zags'. As the angle eases the path swings leftwards taking a more gradual traversing line with mining remains below.

5. Look for the junction with the **Miners' Track** noted on the ascent and marked by an **upright stone pillar**. This path descends down a wide scree gully to the shore of **Glaslyn**. (Avoid a path which breaks away slightly earlier and takes a more diagonal line passing close to mines before reaching the lake.)

Follow the path along the shore of Glaslyn to the outflow, then descend

beside the stream to **Llyn Llydaw**. Continue along the northern shore of the lake and across the **stone causeway** originally built by miners working in the **Glaslyn Mines** during the nineteenth century.

6. Beyond the causeway the path is virtually level and wide — almost a road — and contours the slopes back to Pen-y-Pass to complete the walk. ♦

Summit buildings

There have been buildings on the summit of Snowdon since at least the early nineteenth century. These catered for visitors who climbed to the summit on pony to view the sunrise. The 'hotel' was little more than a wooden hut. In 1898 the railway replaced ponies and a summit café building was designed by Sir Clough Williams Ellis, the creator of Porthmeirion. In 2009 the latest building to crown the summit — Hafod Eryri — was opened.

Useful Information

Visit Wales

The Visit Wales website covers everything from accommodation and events to attractions and adventure. For information on the area covered by this book, see: **www.visitwales.co.uk**

Snowdonia National Park

The Snowdonia National Park website also has information on things to see and do, plus maps, webcams and news. **www.snowdonia-npa.gov.uk**

Tourist Information Centres

The main TICs provide free information on everything from accommodation and travel to what's on and walking advice.

Betws-y-coed	01690 710426	TIC.BYC@eryri-npa.gov.uk
Beddgelert	01766 890615	TIC.Beddgelert@eryri-npa.gov.uk
Harlech	01766 780658	TIC.Harlech@eryri-npa.gov.uk
Dolgellau	01341 422888	TIC.Dolgellau@eryri-npa.gov.uk
Aberdyfi	01654 767321	TIC.Aberdyfi@eryri-npa.gov.uk

Emergencies

Snowdonia is covered by volunteer mountain rescue teams. In a real emergency:

1. Make a note of your location (with OS grid reference, if possible); the name, age and sex of the casualty; their injuries; how many people are in the group; and your mobile phone number.

2. Call 999 or 112 and ask for the North Wales police, and then for Mountain Rescue.

3. Give them your prepared details.

4. Do NOT change position until contacted by the mountain rescue team.

Weather

The Met Office operates a 24 hour online weather forecast

Follow the link from the National Park website **www.eryri-npa.gov.uk/visiting/your-weather-forecast-service** or see www.metoffice.gov.uk

Newport Community
Learning & Libraries